Can You Find It?

School Days

A Can-You-Find-It Book

by Sarah L. Schuette

PEBBLE
a capstone imprint

Let's Play!

Can you find
these things?

 ladybug

 dragon

 astronaut

 bee

 hamburger

 birdhouse

 butterfly

 ladder

 duck

 pig

Makerspace

Can you find
these things?

 motorcycle

 pencil

 flashlight

 bucket

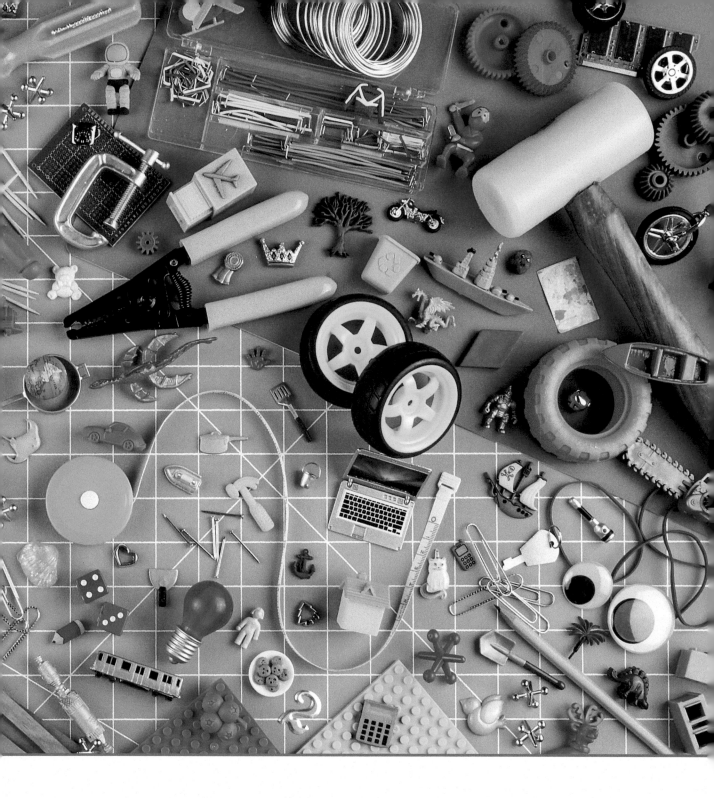

 mouse hat frog spoons cherries flute

ABCs

Can you find
these things?

horseshoe

flamingo

pretzel

pliers

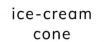 ice-cream cone

 glasses

 screw

 carrots

 chicken

 mug

School Supplies

Can you find these things?

 baseball

 rocket

 tennis racket

 pickle

stapler   toaster   trophy   ice skate   caterpillar   dinosaur

Lunch!

Can you find
these things?

olive

cherries

cake slice

book

eggplant

French fries

spoon

raspberry

avocado

mushroom

School Bus

Can you find these things?

 crayon

 taco

 lollipop

 tennis ball

arrow

alligator

soda
can

starfish

ninja

fish

School Days

Can you find these things?

 apple spaceship narwhal football

 umbrella
 boat
 cookie
 pizza
 paperclip
 bell

Star
Student

Can you find
these things?

 hot dog

 rainbow

 square

 ant

 anchor   heart   skateboard   oval   octopus   Saturn

Making New Friends

Can you find these things?

sandwich

spider

crown

donut

 mitten watermelon sheep unicorn ice pop glasses

How Many?

Can you find
these things?

zebra

tire

moon

hamster

boot

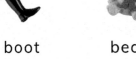
bear

cat

ring

oar

horse

Create It!

Can you find
these things?

 fish

 chain saw

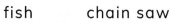 banana

 wagon

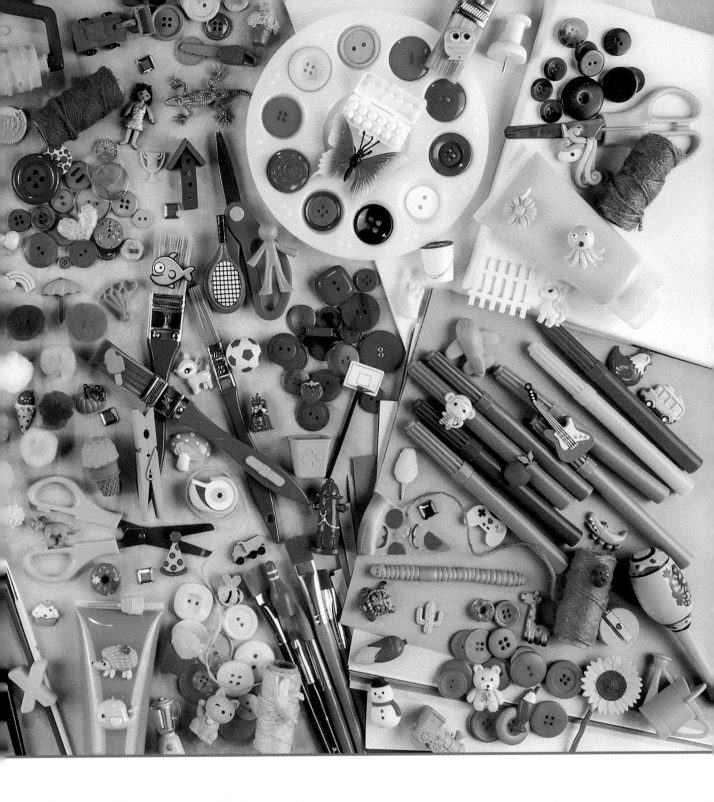

  spray bottle

 lighthouse

 pear

shirt

 rose

 gift

In the Library

Can you find these things?

 owl

 milk jug

 softball

 parrot

sneakers

lock

shark

llama

tent

acorn

Teacher's Desk

Can you find these things?

traffic cone

train

skunk

elephant

 globe

 fishing pole

 tissue box

screwdriver

 key

 guitar

Challenge Puzzle

It's About Time!

Can you find these things?

tulip

pail

pineapple

panda

Turn the page for the answer key!

    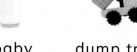

baby bottle   dump truck   bicycle   rabbit   sunflower   shoe

Challenge Puzzle: It's About Time! Answer Key

Psst! Did you know that Pebs the Pebble was hiding
in EVERY PUZZLE in this book?

It's true! Go back and look!

Look for other books in this series:

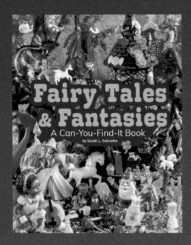

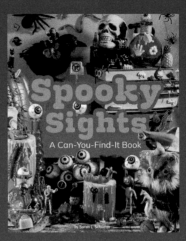

The author dedicates this book to her mom and most favorite teacher of all, Jane Schuette.

Pebble Sprout is published by Pebble, an imprint of Capstone.
1710 Roe Crest Drive, North Mankato, Minnesota 56003
www.capstonepub.com

Library of Congress Cataloging-in-Publication Data is available on the Library of Congress website.
Names: Schuette, Sarah L., 1976- author.
Title: School days : a can-you-find-it book / by Sarah L. Schuette.
Description: North Mankato : Pebble, [2020] | Series: Can you find it? | Audience: Ages 4-8 (provided by Pebble) Identifiers: LCCN 2019057500 (print) | LCCN 2019057499 (ebook) |
ISBN 9781977122582 (library binding) | ISBN 9781977126245 (paperback) | ISBN 9781977123107 (eBook PDF)
Subjects: LCSH: Schools—Juvenile literature. | Special days—Juvenile literature. | Picture puzzles—Juvenile literature. Classification: LCC LB1556 .S383 2020 (ebook) | LCC LB1556 (print) | DDC 793.73—dc23
LC record available at https://lccn.loc.gov/2019057500

Image Credits
All photos by Capstone Studio: Karon Dubke

Editorial Credits
Shelly Lyons, editor; Heidi Thompson, designer; Marcy Morin, set stylist; Morgan Walters, media researcher; Kathy McColley, production specialist